The
Sexton's
Tale
By
THEO. TILTON
HARLEY.

THE

SEXTON'S TALE,

AND OTHER POEMS.

BY

THEODORE TILTON.

NEW YORK:
SHELDON AND COMPANY.
1867.

STEREOTYPED AT THE

BOSTON STEREOTYPE FOUNDRY,

4 Spring Lane.

C. S. WESTCOTT & Co., Printers, 79 John Street, N. Y.

TO

E. R. T.

CONTENTS.

POEMS.

THE SEXTON'S TALE.

SCENE.—*An old English Churchyard.*

PERSONS.—*An aged Sexton (formerly a Duke's henchman) pointing out graves to a Stranger.*

TIME.—*Thirteenth Century.*

I.

A KNIGHT, sir, from the Holy Land
Came back to claim my Lady's hand.
[This grave is his where now we stand.]

II.

My Lady's sire, the Duke, had said
The Knight and she should never wed.
[How thick the leaves are where we tread!]

III.

A maid who knows her father's will,
And weds against it, comes to ill.
[Stand here — the winter wind is chill.]

IV.

Now I, for one, am bold to say
A maid should have her will and way
In what concerns her wedding-day.

V.

So when the Duke took helm and lance,
And went to tournaments in France,
My Lady saw her golden chance.

VI.

If once the holy knot were tied,
The Duke, nor all the world beside,
Could part the bridegroom from his bride.

VII.

Along the wedding-path were strown
So many buds and roses blown,
Their happy feet touched not a stone.

VIII.

Now how it came, I cannot tell,
But never such ill-hap befell
The ringing of a wedding-bell.

IX.

For while the priest was at the prayer,
The Duke — the devil knows from where! —
Uprose behind the married pair!

X.

One faces winter, though it blows
And frosts one's breath, — and so we rose
And faced him, though our pulses froze!

XI.

The Duke had sword, and shield, and squire;
The Knight was in his wedding-tire;
They fronted, and their eyes flashed fire!

XII.

Then turned the father toward his child,
And touched her wedding-ring, and smiled.
The Duke (we thought) was reconciled.

XIII.

Quoth he, "My daughter and my son,
Against my will the deed is done;
But twain, whom God hath joined, are one.

XIV.

"Now follow to my castle-hall!
Come, old and young! come, great and small!
A feast awaiteth one and all!"

XV.

It was a lie the villain told!
His soul was to the devil sold!
[*Hic jacet*—here's his rotten mould!]

XVI.

Thus cheated forward to their fate,
The lovers reached the castle-gate,
Where, hid behind it, lay in wait

XVII.

Five henchmen, who—like hounds in check,
Yet daring, at their master's beck,
To grip a lion by the neck—

XVIII.

Sprang at the Knight, and girt him round,
And hurled him headlong to the ground,
And held him like a lion bound!

XIX.

Then cried the Duke — the double-faced! —
"Thy wife shall be a virgin chaste,
And never in thine arms embraced!

XX.

"This wall shall thee and thine divide,
And make thee bridegroom to a bride
Who shall not slumber at thy side!"

XXI.

The Knight, unhanded, never spoke,
But stood as dumb as when an oak
Replies not to the thunder-stroke.

XXII.

I watched my Lady's color fade;
She fainted to a ghostly shade,
And lay as if her grave were made.

XXIII.

Whereat the Duke to me made sign
To lift her with these arms of mine,
And bear her in, and give her wine.

XXIV.

I raised my Lady, all aghast,
And loud behind me, as I passed,
The gate was slammed, and bolted fast.

XXV.

The groom without, the bride within!—
To sunder whom was mortal sin—
For wedded hearts are more than kin.

XXVI.

[This gust blows through and through one's
cloak:
Just step in shelter of this oak.]
Well, when at last my Lady spoke,

XXVII.

She gave a look so full of fright,
And wept in such a widowed plight,
My soul was melted at the sight.

XXVIII.

But woman's love is wondrous strong;
I helped to right my Lady's wrong;
I shall not make the story long.

XXIX.

On Christmas night, the castle-wall
Was hung with holly, and the hall
Was thronged with guests: she fled them all,

XXX.

And, mutely as a mouse could stir,
To me came down in hood and fur,
And asked, Was I a friend to her?

XXXI.

I made obeisance on my knee.
"May Heaven be thy reward!" said she;
"Unlock the gate, and set me free!"

XXXII.

O, when is ever seen or heard
Such majesty of look or word
As when a woman's soul is stirred!

XXXIII.

While there she stood to plead her case,
She bore so high and grand a grace,
I grew abashed before her face.

XXXIV.

I durst have swung that castle-gate
Wide open then, had Death and Fate
Made groans if any hinge should grate!

XXXV.

I slid the bolt at her command,
And she — the Lady of the Land! —
Caught up and kissed this rough old hand!

XXXVI.

I heard a champing horse outside:
The bridegroom waited for his bride:
"God speed," I cried, "the wedding-ride!"

XXXVII.

A single thing I hate to say:
It pricks me to this very day:
The Knight threw back his purse for pay.

XXXVIII.

It lies there yet, for aught I know!
The hand my Lady honored so
Disdained to lift a bribe so low.

XXXIX.

The Duke was wroth, but never knew
Who drew the bolt to let her through.
[There, that's my Lady's, next to you!]

XL.

Ah, well! the ways of God are right:
My Lady's babe was born at night:
My Lady died at morning-light.

XLI.

Sweet, fragile stalk! that grew too rare
The burden of its bud to bear,
And broke while blossoming so fair!

XLII.

In one white sheet they both were dressed;
The babe was placed upon her breast;
And so we laid the twain to rest.

XLIII.

The Knight, heart-broken, hardly stayed
Until my Lady's mound was made,
But joined King Richard's great crusade.

XLIV.

Three summers afterward, one morn,
A pilgrim, pale and travel-worn,—
And in his hand a palm-branch borne,—

XLV.

Walked in the churchyard here alone,
And at my Lady's grave, moss-grown,
Threw down the trophy on the stone;

XLVI.

Then crossed himself, and walked away;
And just a month from that same day,
I wrapped a shroud about his clay.

XLVII.

So here's the bride, and there's the groom:
But come and see my Lady's tomb
When summer roses are in bloom:

XLVIII.

For now the winter wrongs the dead,
To plant the pillow of her bed
With only thorns about her head.

XLIX.

The groom lies parted from the bride;
But Life and Love, that here divide,
Are joined upon the other side!

THE GREAT BELL ROLAND.*

SUGGESTED BY PRESIDENT LINCOLN'S FIRST CALL FOR VOLUNTEERS.

I.

TOLL! Roland, toll!
In old St. Bavon's tower,
At midnight hour,
The great bell Roland spoke;
And all who slept in Ghent awoke.

*The famous bell Roland of Ghent, as Motley relates, was an object of great affection to the people, because it rang to arm them when Liberty was in danger.

What meant the thunder-stroke?
Why trembled wife and maid?
Why caught each man his blade?
Why echoed every street
With tramp of thronging feet,
  All flying to the city's wall?
  It was the warning call
That Freedom stood in peril of a foe!
And timid hearts grew bold
Whenever Roland tolled,
And every hand a sword could hold,
And every arm could bend a bow!
  So acted men
  Like patriots then —
Three hundred years ago!

II.

Toll! Roland, toll!
Bell never yet was hung,
Between whose lips there swung
So grand a tongue!
If men be patriots still,
At thy first sound
True hearts will bound,
Great souls will thrill!
Then toll, and let thy test
Try each man's breast,
And let him stand confessed!

III.

Toll! Roland, toll!
Not now in old St. Bavon's tower—
Not now at midnight hour—

Not now from River Scheldt to Zuyder Zee;
But here! — this side the sea! —
Toll here, in broad, bright day!
  For not by night awaits
  A foe without the gates,
But perjured friends within betray,
  And do the deed at noon!
    Toll! Roland, toll!
  Thy sound is not too soon!
To arms! Ring out the Leader's call!
    Toll! Roland, toll! —
Till cottager from cottage-wall
  Snatch pouch, and powder-horn, and
      gun —
  The heritage of sire to son,
  Ere half of Freedom's work was done!
    Toll! Roland, toll! —
  Till swords from scabbards leap!

Toll! Roland, toll!
What tears can widows weep
Less bitter than when brave men fall?
Toll! Roland, toll!
In shadowed hut and hall
Shall lie the soldier's pall,
And hearts shall break while graves are filled!
Amen! So God hath willed!
And may His grace anoint us all!

IV.

Toll! Roland, toll!
The Dragon on thy tower
Stands sentry to this hour;
And Freedom now is safe in Ghent;
And merrier bells now ring;

And in the land's serene content,
Men shout, "God save the King!"—
Until the skies are rent!
So let it be!—
A kingly King is he
Who keeps his people free!
Toll! Roland, toll!
Ring out across the sea!
No longer They, but We,
Have now such need of thee!
Toll! Roland, toll!
Nor ever let thy throat
Keep dumb its warning note
Till Freedom's perils be outbraved!
Toll! Roland, toll!—
Till Freedom's flag, wherever waved,
Shall shadow not a man enslaved!

Toll! Roland, toll!—
From Northern lake to Southern strand!
Toll! Roland, toll!—
Till friend and foe, at thy command,
Shall clasp once more each other's hand,
And shout, one-voiced, "God save the land!"
And love the land that God hath saved!
Toll! Roland, toll!

APRIL 16, 1861.

THE TRUE CHURCH.

I.

ONE Sabbath morn I roamed astray,
And asked a Pilgrim for the way:

"O, tell me, whither shall I search,
That I may find the one true church?"

He answered, "Search the world around;
The one true church is never found;

"Yon ivy on the abbey wall
Makes fair the falsest church of all."

But fearing he had told me wrong,
I cried, "Behold the entering throng!"

He answered, "If a church be true,
It hath not many, but a few!"

Around a font the people pressed,
And crossed themselves on brow and breast.

"A cross so light to bear," he cried,
"Is not of Christ the Crucified! —

"Each forehead, frowning, sheds it off:
Christ's cross abides through scowl and scoff!"

We entered at the open door,
And saw men kneeling on the floor; —

Faint candles, by the daylight dimmed,
As if by foolish virgins trimmed;—

Fair statues of the saints, as white
As now their robes are, in God's light;—

Stained windows, casting down a beam,
Like Jacob's ladder in the dream.

The Pilgrim gazed from nave to roof,
And, frowning, uttered this reproof:—

"Alas! who is it understands
God's temple is not made with hands?"

II.

We walked in ferns so wet with dew
They plashed our garments trailing through,

And came upon a church whose dome
Upheld a cross, but not for Rome.

We brushed a cobweb from a pane,
And watched the service in the fane.

"Do prayers," he asked, "the more avail,
If offered at an altar-rail?

"Does water, sprinkled from a bowl,
Wash any sin from any soul?

"Do tongues that taste the bread and wine
Speak truer after such a sign?"

Just then, upon a maple spray,
Two orioles perched, and piped a lay, —

Until the gold beneath their throats
Shook molten in their mellow notes.

Resounding from the church, a psalm
Rolled, quivering, through the outer calm.

"Both choirs," said I, "are in accord,
For both give praises to the Lord."

"The birds," he answered, "chant a song
Without a note of sin or wrong:

"The church's anthem is a strain
Of human guilt and mortal pain."

The orioles and the organ ceased,
And in the pulpit rose the priest.

The Pilgrim whispered in my ear,
"It profits not to tarry here."

"He speaks no error," answered I;
"He teaches that the living die;

"The dead arise; and both are true;
Both wholesome doctrines; neither new."

The Pilgrim said, "He strikes a blow
At wrongs that perished long ago;

"But covers with a shielding phrase
The living sins of present days."

We turned away among the tombs—
A tangled place of briers and blooms.

I spelled the legends on the stones:
Beneath reposed the martyrs' bones,—

The bodies which the rack once brake
In witness for the dear Lord's sake,—

The ashes gathered from the pyres
Of saints whose souls went up through fires.

The Pilgrim murmured as we passed,
"So gained they all the crown at last.

"Men lose it now through looking back
To find it at the stake and rack.

"The rack and stake are old with grime;
God's touchstone is the living time."

III.

We passed where poplars, gaunt and tall,
Let twice their length of shadow fall.

Then rose a meeting-house in view,
Of bleached and weather-beaten hue.

Men plain of garb and pure of heart
Divided church and world apart.

Nor did they vex the silent air
With any sound of hymn or prayer.

God's finger to their lips they pressed,
Till each man kissed it, and was blessed.

I asked, "Is this the true church, then?"
He answered, "Nay, a sect of men:

"And sects, that lock their doors in pride,
Shut God and half his saints outside.

"The gates of Heaven, the Scriptures say,
Stand open wide by night and day:

"So then, to enter, is there need
To carry key of church or creed?"

IV.

Still following where the highway led,
Till elms made arches overhead,

We saw a spire, and weathercock,
And snow-white church upon a rock,—

A rock where, centuries before,
Came sea-tossed pilgrims to the shore.

My sandals straightway I unbound,
Because the place was holy ground.

I cried, "One church at last I find,
That fetters not the human mind."

"This church," said he, "is like the rest;
For all are good, but none is best."

V.

Then far from every church we strayed—
Save Nature's pillared aisles of shade.

The squirrels ran to see us pass,
And God's sweet breath was on the grass.

I challenged all the creeds, and sought
What truth, or lie, or both, they taught.

I asked, "Had Augustine a fault?"
The Pilgrim gazed at Heaven's high vault,

And answered, "Can a mortal eye
Contain the sphere of all the sky?"

I said, "The circle is too wide."
"God's truth is wider!" he replied.

"Though Augustine was on his knee,
He saw how little he could see;

"Though Luther sought with burning heart,
He caught the glory but in part;

"Though Calvin opened wide his soul,
He comprehended not the whole.

"Not Luther, Calvin, Augustine
Saw visions such as I have seen."

While yet he spake, a rapture stole
Through all my body and my soul.

I looked upon his holy brow,
Entreating, "Tell me, who art THOU?"

But such a splendor filled the place,
I knew it was the Lord's own face!

I was a sinner, and afraid!
I knelt in dust, and thus I prayed:—

"O Christ the Lord! end Thou my search,
And lead me to the one true church."

He spake as never man may speak,—
"The one true church thou shalt not seek:

"Seek thou, forevermore, instead,
To find the one true Christ, its Head!"

The Lord then vanished from my sight,
And left me standing in the light.

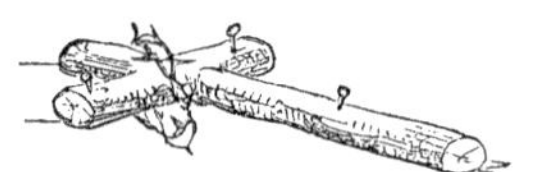

THE MYSTERY OF NATURE.

I.

THE works of God are fair for nought
  Unless our eyes, in seeing,
See, hidden in the thing, the thought
  That animates its being.

II.

The outward form is not the whole,
  But every part is moulded
To image forth an inward soul
  That dimly is unfolded.

III.

The shadow, pictured in the lake
By every tree that trembles,
Is cast for more than just the sake
Of that which it resembles.

IV.

The dew falls nightly, not alone
Because the meadows need it,
But hath an errand of its own
To human souls that heed it.

V.

The stars are lighted in the skies
Not merely for their shining,
But, like the looks of loving eyes,
Have meanings worth divining.

VI.

The waves that moan along the shore,
  The winds that sigh in blowing,
Are sent to teach a mystic lore
  Which men are wise in knowing.

VII.

The clouds around the mountain peak,
  The rivers in their winding,
Have secrets which, to all who seek,
  Are precious in the finding.

VIII.

Thus Nature dwells within our reach,
  But, though we stand so near her,
We still interpret half her speech
  With ears too dull to hear her.

IX.

Whoever, at the coarsest sound,
 Still listens for the finest,
Shall hear the noisy world go round
 To music the divinest.

X.

Whoever yearns to see aright
 Because his heart is tender,
Shall catch a glimpse of heavenly light
 In every earthly splendor.

XI.

So, since the universe began,
 And till it shall be ended,
The soul of Nature, soul of Man,
 And soul of God are blended!

THE KING'S RING.

I.

ONCE in Persia reigned a King,
Who upon his signet ring
Graved a maxim true and wise,
Which, if held before his eyes,
Gave him counsel, at a glance,
Fit for every change or chance:
Solemn words, and these are they:
"Even this shall pass away!"

II.

Trains of camels through the sand
Brought him gems from Samarcand;
Fleets of galleys through the seas
Brought him pearls to rival these.
But he counted little gain
Treasures of the mine or main.
"What is wealth?" the King would say;
"'Even this shall pass away.'"

III.

In the revels of his court,
At the zenith of the sport,
When the palms of all his guests
Burned with clapping at his jests,
He, amid his figs and wine,
Cried, "O loving friends of mine!
Pleasure comes, but not to stay:
'Even this shall pass away.'"

IV.

Lady fairest ever seen
Was the bride he crowned his queen.
Pillowed on the marriage-bed,
Whispering to his soul, he said,
"Though a bridegroom never pressed
Dearer bosom to his breast,
Mortal flesh must come to clay:
'Even this shall pass away.'"

V.

Fighting on a furious field,
Once a javelin pierced his shield.
Soldiers with a loud lament
Bore him bleeding to his tent.
Groaning from his tortured side,
"Pain is hard to bear," he cried,
"But with patience day by day,
'Even this shall pass away.'"

VI.

Towering in the public square
Twenty cubits in the air,
Rose his statue carved in stone.
Then the King, disguised, unknown,
Gazing at his sculptured name,
Asked himself, "And what is fame?
Fame is but a slow decay:
'Even this shall pass away.'"

VII.

Struck with palsy, sere and old,
Waiting at the Gates of Gold,
Spake he with his dying breath,
"Life is done, but what is Death?"
Then, in answer to the King,
Fell a sunbeam on his ring,
Showing by a heavenly ray —
"Even this shall pass away."

THE PARSON'S COURTSHIP.

I.

THE story, as I heard it told,
  I fashion into idle rhyme,
To show that, though the heart grows old,
  Yet love abides in golden prime.

II.

An aged parson, on his mare,
  Was riding where his heart inclined,
Yet wore a sober look and air,
  As one who had a troubled mind.

III.

For, when he passed the graveyard gate,
His eyes grew dim with sudden tears
In looking at a slab of slate,
Where lay his wife of other years.

IV.

She, dying, said it wronged the dead
To make a wedding on a grave:
The words kept ringing in his head,
And great bewilderment they gave.

V.

He longed to make a second choice,
For every Sunday in the choir
He heard the Widow Churchill's voice,
Until she grew his heart's desire.

VI.

The parson's passion, unconfessed,
  Like smouldered heat within him burned,
Which never once the widow guessed,
  Or haply it had been returned.

VII.

With hazel branch the mare was switched,
  And cantered down the winding road,
And underneath a tree was hitched,
  At Captain Churchill's old abode.

VIII.

The dame was busy sifting flour,
  Nor heard the comer till he said,
"Be praise to that Almighty Power
  Who giveth man his daily bread!"

IX.

The widow — caught by such a guest
  In just her linsey-woolsey gown,
Instead of in her Sunday best —
  Dropped bashfully her eyelids down.

X.

Then spake her suitor to her face —
  "I have a solemn word to say,
Whereto is need of heavenly grace;
  So, Widow Churchill, let us pray!"

XI.

Devoutly did the couple kneel —
  The parson at the rocking-chair,
The widow at the spinning-wheel —
  And this the burden of the prayer: —

XII.

He mourned for uncommitted sin,
  Implored a grace on all mankind,
And asked that love might enter in
  And sweetly move the widow's mind.

XIII.

Uprising from his prayerful knees,
  "I seek a wife," the parson said,
"And, finding thee, if God shall please,
  Nor thou deny, then let us wed!"

XIV.

The widow started with surprise
  (For women old are women still),
And answered, lifting not her eyes,
  "I seek to do the heavenly will."

XV.

The heavenly will was plain indeed,
  And pointed to the flowery yoke,
For love is not the human need
  Of young alone, but aged folk.

XVI.

One day, when asters were in bloom,
  There came a throng from far and near,
To wish the joy of bride and groom,
  And eat and drink the wedding-cheer.

XVII.

That night, beside the bridal bed,
  Up spoke the bride in tender tone,
"I hold a message from the dead,
  And time has come to make it known:

XVIII.

"The years are twelve, this very day,
  Since she whose title now is mine,
The night before she passed away,
  Bequeathed to me this written line:—

XIX.

"'To thee, O friend of all my life,
  I vow before my strength be spent,
That should he wed another wife,
  If thou art she, I rest content.'"

XX.

He gazed upon the well-known hand,
  Thought backward of the bygone years,
Thought forward of the heavenly land,
  And answered not a word for tears.

XXI.

A hallowed honeymoon they passed,
  And both grew young in growing old,
Till, sweetly fading out at last,
  They left the tale that I have told.

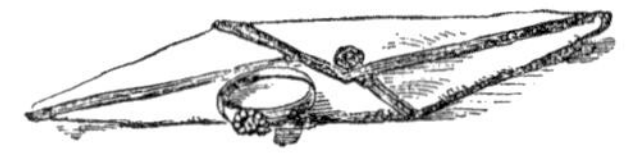

NO AND YES.

I.

I WATCHED her at her spinning,
And this was my beginning
Of wooing and of winning.

II.

So cruel, so uncaring,
So scornful was her bearing,
She set me half despairing.

III.

Yet sorry wit one uses,
Who loves, and thinks he loses
Because a maid refuses.

IV.

Love prospers in the making
By help of all its aching,
And quaking, and heart-breaking.

V.

A woman's first denying
Betokens her complying
Upon a second trying.

VI.

When first I said in pleading,
"Behold, my love lies bleeding!" —
She shook her head unheeding.

VII.

But when again I told her,
And blamed her growing colder,
She dropped against my shoulder.

VIII.

Then, with her eyes of splendor,
She gave a look so tender,
I knew she would surrender!

IX.

So down the lane I led her,
And while her cheek grew redder,
I sued outright to wed her.

X.

Good end from bad beginning!
My wooing came to winning!
And still I watch her spinning!

THE CAPTAIN'S WIFE.

I.

WE gathered roses, Blanche and I, for
little Madge one morning:
"Like every soldier's wife," said Blanche,
"I dread a soldier's fate."
Her voice a little trembled then, as under
some forewarning.
A soldier galloped up the lane, and halted
at the gate.

II.

"Which house is Malcolm Blake's?" he
cried; "a letter for his sister!"

And when I thanked him, Blanche inquired,
"But none for me, his wife?"
The soldier played with Madge's curls, and, stooping over, kissed her:
"Your father was my captain, child! — I loved him as my life!"

III.

Then suddenly he galloped off, and left the rest unspoken.
I burst the seal, and Blanche exclaimed, "What makes you tremble so?"
What answer did I dare to make? How should the news be broken?
I could not shield her from the stroke, yet tried to ease the blow.

IV.

"A battle in the swamps," I said; "our
men were brave, but lost it."
And, pausing there, — "The note," I said,
"is not in Malcolm's hand."
And first a flush flamed through her face,
and then a shadow crossed it:
"Read quick, dear May! — read all, I
pray! — and let me understand!"

V.

I did not read it as it stood, but tempered
so the phrases
As not at first to hint the worst, — kept
back the fatal word,
And half retold his gallant charge, his
shout, his comrades' praises, —
Till, like a statue carved in stone, she neither
spoke nor stirred!

VI.

O, never yet a woman's heart was frozen so
completely! —
So unbaptized with helping tears! — so
passionless and dumb!
Spell-bound she stood, and motionless, till
little Madge said sweetly,
"Dear mother, is the battle done? and will
my father come?"

VII.

I laid my hand on Madge's lips, and led her
to her playing.
Poor Blanche! the winter in her cheek was
snowy like her name!
What could she do but kneel, and pray, and
linger at her praying?
O Christ! when other heroes die, moan
other wives the same?

VIII.

Must other women's hearts yet break, to
keep the Cause from failing?
God pity our brave lovers then, who face
the battle's blaze!
And pity wives in widowhood! — But is it
unavailing?
O Lord! give Freedom first, then Peace! —
and unto Thee be praise!

THE CLOUD OF WITNESSES.

"Are they not all ministering spirits?"

I.

I LEANED upon a burial urn,
And thought how life is but a day,
And how the nations, each in turn,
Have lived and passed away.

II.

The earth is peopled with the dead,
Who live again in deathless hosts,
And come and go with noiseless tread —
A universe of ghosts.

III.

They follow after flying ships,
  They flicker through the city's marts,
They hear the cry of human lips —
  The beat of human hearts.

IV.

They linger not around their tombs,
  But far from churchyards keep aloof,
To dwell in old familiar rooms
  Beneath the household roof.

V.

They waken men at morning light,
  They cheer them in their daily care,
They bring a weary world at night
  To bend the knee in prayer.

VI.

Their errand is of God assigned
  To comfort sorrow till it cease,
And in the dark and troubled mind
  To light the lamp of peace.

VII.

There is a language, whispered low,
  Whereby to mortal ears they speak,
To which we answer by a glow
  That kindles in the cheek.

VIII.

Dear shadows, fairer than the day,
  With heavenly light they wrap us round,
Wherein we walk a gilded way,
  And over holy ground.

IX.

O, what a wondrous life is theirs! —
  To fling away the mortal frame,
Yet keep the human loves, and cares,
  And yearnings still the same!

X.

O, what a wondrous life is ours! —
  To dwell within this earthly range,
Yet parley with the heavenly powers —
  Two worlds in interchange!

XI.

O, balm of grief! — to understand
  That whom our eyes behold no more
Still clasp us with as true a hand
  As in the flesh before!

XII.

No longer in a gloom profound
  Let Memory, like a mourner craped,
Sit weeping by an empty mound
  Whose captive hath escaped!

XIII.

So, turning from the burial urn,
  I thought how life has double worth,
If men be only wise to learn
  That heaven is on the earth.

THE FLIGHT FROM THE CONVENT.

I.

I SEE the star-lights quiver,
Like jewels in the river;
The bank is hid with sedge;
What if I slip the edge?
I thought I knew the way
By night as well as day:
How soon a lover goes astray!

II.

The place is somewhat lonely —
I mean, for just one only.
I brought the boat ashore
An hour ago, or more.
Well, I will sit and wait;

She fixed the hour at eight:
Good angels! bring her not too late!

III.

To-morrow's tongues that name her
Will hardly dare to blame her:
A lily still is white
Through all the dark of night:
The morning sun shall show
A bride as pure as snow,
Whose wedding all the world shall know.

IV.

O God! that I should gain her!
But what can so detain her?
Hist, yelping cur! thy bark
Will fright her in the dark.
What! striking nine? that's fast!
Is some one walking past?
Oho! so thou art come at last!

V.

Now, why thy long delaying?
Alack! thy beads and praying!
If thou, a saint, dost hope
To kneel and kiss the Pope,
Then I, a sinner, know
Where sweeter kisses grow —
Nay, now, just once before we go!

VI.

Nay, twice, and by St. Peter
The second was the sweeter!
Quick, now, and in the boat!
Good by, old tower and moat!
May mildew from the sky
Drop blindness on the eye
That lurks to watch our going by!

VII.

O saintly maid! I told thee
No convent walls should hold thee.
Look! yonder comes the moon!
We started not too soon.
See how we pass that mill!
What! is the night too chill?
Then I must fold thee closer still!

THE FISHER'S CHILD.

I.

I WEAVE a tale of old and new;
The half a fact, the rest a dream;
Yet many dreams are wondrous true,
However strange they seem.

II.

So silent was the summer day,
That one could hear the far-off bees,
Till winds from over fields of hay
Came down to rough the seas.

III.

A fisher brought his nets to land,
  And just above the water's reach
Drew out his boat upon the sand,
  And hurried from the beach.

IV.

Along a reedy water-edge,
  His little son ran up and down,
And, breaking off the spears of sedge,
  Entwined them for a crown.

V.

Now, when the urchin spied the craft,
  He clambered up the side in glee,
And tossed his laurelled head, and laughed,
  And wished himself at sea.

VI.

The boat, amid the watery roar,
  Was like a warning finger, laid
Across the lips of sea and shore,
  To hush the noise they made.

VII.

A breaker, with a headlong swell,
  Ran up around it where it lay,
And rolled so high that when it fell
  It launched the boat away.

VIII.

The poplar trees grew tall and green
  Between the fisher and the tide,
And sadder sight was never seen
  Than there they stood to hide.

IX.

By rushing winds, the drifting hull
  Was blown beyond the harbor-light,
Till, seaward, like a flying gull,
  It dwindled out of sight.

X.

The father never called his child
  Until the west was all aflame,
And then, except an echo wild,
  No voice in answer came.

XI.

Whereat, as with a giant's hand,
  The frantic fisher seized a boat,
And dragged it down the griping sand,
  And through the surf afloat.

XII.

He pulled his oars for thrice a league,
And down his brawny beard ran sweat,
But not a sinew felt fatigue,
For hope inspired him yet.

XIII.

The mantle of the night was dark,
Wherein his eyes were folded blind,
And so he chased the truant bark,
To seek, but not to find.

XIV.

At last his strength was overspent,
And down against his panting breast
His hot, bewildered head he bent,
And swooned, and lay at rest.

XV.

He dreamed that through a yawning wave
  A child, with sea-grass on his head,
Went down within a boundless grave,
  To wander with the dead:

XVI.

Thence rising to a wondrous land,
  The human creature grew divine:
And when the fisher waved his hand,
  The child gave back a sign.

XVII.

The dreamer woke with sudden start,
  And, shuddering in the chilly dew,
Knew well, by token in his heart,
  The vision must be true.

XVIII.

In sorrow homeward he returned,
And sank aweary in his chair,
And, gazing where the embers burned,
Beheld an angel there!

XIX.

And in the old familiar place
Which on the earth it loved the best,
A figure with a shining face
Is still the fisher's guest.

XX.

O, pleasantest of mortal things! —
That angels dwell in homes on earth,
Where silently, with folded wings,
They tarry by the hearth!

A LAYMAN'S CONFESSION OF FAITH.

AS other men have creeds, so I have mine:
I keep the holy faith in God, in man,
And in the angels ministrant between.

I hold to one true church of all true souls;
Whose churchly seal is neither bread, nor wine,
Nor laying on of hands, nor holy oil,
But only the anointing of God's grace.

I hate all kings, and caste, and rank of birth:
For all the sons of men are sons of God;

Nor limps a beggar but is nobly born;
Nor wears a slave a yoke, nor czar a crown,
That makes him less or more than just a
man.

I love my country and her righteous cause:
So dare I not keep silent of her sin;
And after Freedom, may her bells ring
Peace!

I love one woman with a holy fire,
Whom I revere as priestess of my house;
I stand with wondering awe before my
babes,
Till they rebuke me to a nobler life;
I keep a faithful friendship with my friend,
Whom loyally I serve before myself;
I lock my lips too close to speak a lie;

I wash my hands too white to touch a bribe;
I owe no man a debt I cannot pay—
Except the love that men should always
owe.

Withal, each day, before the blessed Heaven,
I open wide the chambers of my soul,
And pray the Holy Ghost to enter in.

Thus reads the fair confession of my faith,
So crossed with contradictions by my life,
That now may God forgive the written lie!
Yet still, by help of Him who helpeth men,
I face two worlds, and fear not life nor death!
O Father! lead me by Thy hand! Amen.

1862.

THE LOTUS PLANTER.

I.

A BRAHMIN on a lotus pod
Once wrote the holy name of God.

II.

Then, planting it, he asked in prayer
For some new fruit, unknown and fair.

III.

A slave near by, who bore a load,
Fell fainting on the dusty road.

IV.

The Brahmin, pitying, straightway ran
And lifted up the fallen man.

V.

The deed scarce done, he looked aghast
At touching one beneath his caste.

VI.

"Behold!" he cried, "I stand unclean:
My hands have clasped the vile and mean!"

VII.

God saw the shadow on his face,
And wrought a miracle of grace.

VIII.

The buried seed arose from death,
And bloomed and fruited at His breath.

IX.

The stalk bore up a leaf of green,
Whereon these mystic words were seen:—

X.

FIRST COUNT MEN ALL OF EQUAL CASTE;
THEN COUNT THYSELF THE LEAST AND LAST.

XI.

The Brahmin, with bewildered brain,
Beheld the will of God writ plain!

XII.

Transfigured in a sudden light,
The slave stood sacred in his sight.

XIII.

Thenceforth within the Brahmin's mind
Abode good will for all mankind.

THE CROWN OF THORNS.

I.

THY head was crowned with thorns:
  What crown shall be for mine?
Are there for me no scoffs, no scorns,
  Since only such were Thine?

II.

Or, having named Thy name,
  Shall I no burden take?
And is there left no wound, no shame,
  To suffer for Thy sake?

III.

Unscourged of any whip,
  Unpierced of any sting,—
O Christ, how weak my fellowship
  With Thy strong suffering!

IV.

Yet Thy dread sacrifice
  So fills my soul with woe,
That all the fountains of mine eyes
  Well up and overflow.

V.

The spear that pierced Thy side
  Gave wounds to more than Thee.
Within my soul, O Crucified,
  Thy cross is laid on me!

VI.

And as Thy rocky tomb
  Was in a garden fair,
Where round about stood flowers in bloom,
  To sweeten all the air, —

VII.

So, in my heart of stone
  I sepulchre Thy death,
While thoughts of Thee, like roses blown,
  Bring sweetness in their breath.

VIII.

Arise not, O my Dead! —
  As He whom Mary sought,
And found an empty tomb instead,
  Her spices all for nought, —

IX.

O Lord, not so depart
  From my enshrining breast,
But lie anointed in a heart
  That by Thy death is blest!

X.

Or if Thou shalt arise,
  Abandon not Thy grave,
But bear it with Thee to the skies—
  A heart that Thou shalt save!

THE SAILOR'S WEDDING.

I.

LOITERING ship!" a sailor cried,
"Now speed me home to wed my
bride!"
The ship, through flying spray,
Went bounding on her way.

II.

"O midnight bells! my watch is done;
O happy morrow! haste thy sun."
Then down he lay and slept,
And in his dream he wept.

III.

He dreamed that suddenly the waves
Stood fixed and green, like churchyard graves,
And then a mournful bell
Rang out a funeral knell.

IV.

"Land ho!" the deck-watch called, with cheers;
The sleeper wakened from his tears.
"O, day of joy!" he said;
"This night shall I be wed."

V.

With eager feet he leaped ashore,
And stood at Mary's cottage door:
The bride, in white all dressed,
Was in her grave at rest!

THE VICTORY OF LIFE.

I.

I ONCE made search, in hope to find
Abiding peace of mind.

II.

I toiled for riches — as if these
Could bring the spirit ease!

III.

I turned aside to books and lore,
Still baffled as before.

IV.

I tasted then of love, and fame,
    But hungered still the same.

V.

I chose the sweetest paths I knew,
    Where only roses grew.

VI.

Then fell a voice from out the skies,
    With warning in this wise:

VII.

"O my disciple! is it meet
    That roses tempt thy feet?

VIII.

"Thy Master, even for His head,
Had only thorns instead!"

IX.

Then, drawn as by a heavenly grace,
I left the flowery place,

X.

And walked on cutting flints and stones,
And said with tears and groans:

XI.

"O Lord! my feet, where Thou dost lead,
Shall follow, though they bleed!"

XII.

As then I saw He chose my path
For discipline, not wrath,—

XIII.

I walked in weakness, till at length
I suffered unto strength.

XIV.

Yet never were my trials done,
But only new begun.

XV.

For when I learned to cast disdain
Upon some special pain,—

XVI.

He gave me sharper strokes to bear,
And pierced me to despair;

XVII.

Until, so sorely was I pressed,
I broke beneath the test,

XVIII.

And fell within the Tempter's power:
But, in the evil hour,

XIX.

Bound hand and foot, I cried, "O Lord!
Break Thou the threefold cord!"

XX.

And while my soul was at her prayer,
He snatched me from the snare.

XXI.

I then drew nigh the gate of death,
Where, struggling for my breath,

XXII.

I shook my coward knees in fear,
Aghast to stand so near!

XXIII.

Yet while I shivered in the gloom,
Down-gazing in the tomb,

XXIV.

"O Lord!" I cried, "bear Thou my sin,
And I will enter in!"

XXV.

But He by whom my soul was tried
Not yet was satisfied.

XXVI.

For then he crushed me with a blow
Of more than mortal woe, —

XXVII.

Till bitter death had been relief
To my more bitter grief.

XXVIII.

Yet, bleeding, panting, in the dust,
I knew His judgment just;

XXIX.

And as a lark with broken wing
Sometimes has heart to sing, —

XXX.

So I, all shattered, still could raise
To His dear name the praise!

XXXI.

Henceforth I know a holy prayer,
To conquer pain and care.

XXXII.

For when my struggling flesh grows faint,
And murmurs with complaint,

XXXIII.

My spirit cries, "THY WILL BE DONE!"
And finds the victory won!

A WOMAN'S LETTER.

Y friend (mark, only *friend*, and nothing more),
To-night, in parting from you at the door,
I meant to speak what now I haste to write.
You saw me stand awaiting your good night;
You asked me for my lips, — I answered nay;
You then let fall my hand, and fled away.

The rose you gave me, — will it not decay?
Am I a fool, to think that love endures?
I knew a tongue whose words were fair as yours;

If *he* was false, the rest may prove the same.
You too! If this be harsh, am I to blame?
Are bitter things that go by some sweet name
Less bitter? Love is but a sweet-named gall!

A heart can never trust until it knows;
A heart can never know until it trusts;
A heart is never safe that loves at all.
Love is the pain of pains, the woe of woes!
Let women's bosoms turn to marble busts!

You have a right to know; so be it known,—
I have no other heart except a stone!

I have not said that every man deceives;
Nor do I say no woman's heart hath burned,
Like mine, with love, and found the love
returned:

I only know the lesson I have learned!
Since then, I have not loved; I love not
now;
I shall not love again. Not any vow
Which any man may make — not yours
to-day —
Not were it crowned with every bud of
May —
Would change this final answer, which is
Nay!

RED, WHITE, AND BLUE.*

I.

RED Cypress! Thee I pluck to-day.
All flowers have meanings, poets say.
The legend of thy leaf
Is death and grief:
Thou growest for the sake
Of hearts that break.
And since so many hearts have bled,
Thy star hath grown blood-red.
Thee on my breast I wear,
To show a heart bleeds there!

* Written in 1863, when everybody was wearing a rosette of red, white, and blue.

II.

WHITE Rose! Why pluck I not the red?
The red rose is for love;
And love I not my dead?
What speaks the white rose of?
Of love in its despair!
This woe is mine to bear—
So I the white rose wear.

III.

BLUE Harebell! Swing thyself in toll
For a departed soul!
Grief is thy other name;
Grief bendeth down thy head;
Grief boweth mine the same—
Grief for my dead!
But grief, most grieving, is most blest!

O, heart of mine! beat not my breast.
God knoweth best:
So be at rest!

PIERRE CARDINAL'S FAITH.

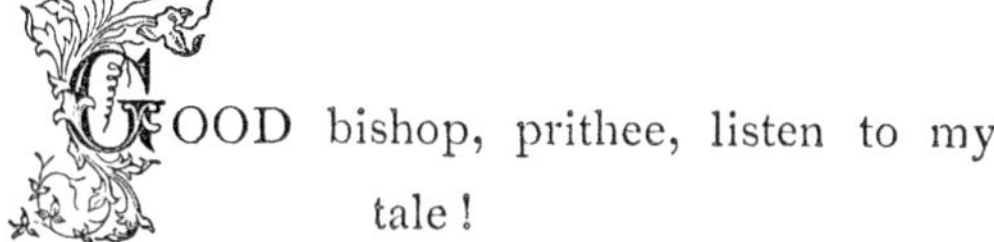
OOD bishop, prithee, listen to my
tale!

Pierre Cardinal, a troubadour of France,
Who bore a hundred years of troubled life,
Fell sick, and called his friends, and spake
these words:
"Now since I have not lived in fear of death,
I trust I shall not die in fear of hell;
Yet when ye shall array me for the grave,
Clench fast this parchment in my folded hand,
That I may read it at the judgment day."

The scroll ran thus — now rotting with his
bones:

"O God! I think the Devil should be slain;
For many a soul were saved to Thee thereby.
Yet since Thy hand hath formed me prone
to sin,
If Thou art wroth at seeing me so made,
Unframe me till I be again unborn.
But if thou wilt not so undo my birth,—
And if I was, and am, and shall be,—then,
O Giver of my hundred years of pain!
Deny me not, I pray, Thy peace at last!
My Father! welcome Thou Thy child.
Amen."

Here stopped the writing, and the minstrel
died.

Good bishop, art thou wise? Then, prithee,
tell,—
Is old Pierre Cardinal in heaven or hell?

THE SOLDIER'S REVENGE.

A. D. 1655.

I.

THIS golden legend first was told
When Swedes and Danes were foes of old.

II.

One morn the Swedes gave way so soon
The battle ended at the noon.

III.

Two foes lay sweltering on the sand,
Each wounded by the other's hand.

IV.

The Swede exclaimed, "O day accurst,
That sees a soldier die of thirst!"

V.

The Dane replied, with anguish wrung,
"My water-flask shall cool thy tongue:

VI.

"I filled it at a mountain spring;
Drink thou to Denmark and the king!

VII.

"But precious loss if any drips;
So hold it steady to thy lips!"

VIII.

The Swede replied, "If thee I kill,
Thy flask is mine to drink my fill!"

IX.

Then drawing poniard from his girth,
He struck a blow, but stabbed the earth.

X.

The Dane exclaimed, "O wretched Swede!
How durst thou do so base a deed!

XI.

"By Heaven! I take revenge, O knave!"
Then snatching back the flask he gave,

XII.

"Thirst thou," he cried, "while I shall
quaff;
Thy throat shall swallow only half!

XIII.

"I meant to bid thee drink the whole:
So curse thy loss, thou dastard soul!"

XIV.

The King of Denmark overheard,
And smiling at the deed and word,

XV.

Proclaimed, in sight of all his train,
"I dub thee knight, O noble Dane!"

XVI.

Uprose a noise of Danish cheers—
Heard yet through twice a hundred years.

XVII.

So every hero hath reward—
Of men, of kings, or of the Lord!

TO THE BRIDE ISABEL.

ENCLOSING A HEART'S-EASE.

O MAIDEN, I who, many miles away,
This way-side letter of remembrance send,
To intercept thy coming wedding-day,
That hastens hither ere the roses end,
Send with it (better than a rose) a flower
Less fair, yet fitter for thy feast;
A flower worth all the gardens of the East,
And rich enough to be thy bridal dower:
For, having heart's-ease, hast thou not enough?

But heart's-ease is a perishable stuff—
A fading flower that hath not long to live—
A mocking gift that is not mine to give.
Yet as I give the emblem, I uplift
A prayer that God will add the perfect gift.

But we who pray know not for what we
plead.
If He who knoweth every human need
Should overrule my gift, and make it vain,
And then bestow instead His gift of pain;
If at His finger-touch thy heart's-ease fade,
And wither into heart-break,—O fair maid!
Who knowest now of love, but not of grief,
Go question all the sorrows of the world,
And thou shalt find that sorrowing love is
chief!

As if a wedding-tress should burst its braid,
Or twisted ringlet droop and hang uncurled,
And shake its orange-blossoms to the ground,
So love at last may loose what first it bound,
And drop the joys wherewith it once was
crowned.

But as a bird that hath a heavenward wing
May shed a plume, yet shall not cease to
sing,
So love, despite her losses, waxeth strong,
And bears above them all a cheery song.

When thou, like other brides whose hearts
have burned
With over-joy of love, hast also learned,
And wept in learning, that through all the
years,

Love often hath her bosom pierced of spears,
Learn thou, by discipline of thorn and sting,
That sorrow also is a sacred thing.
There never yet was any wedding-ring
That did not make a marriage unto tears.
When thou this fading flower away shalt
fling,
May love, that hath no earthly sorrow, bring
Thy bosom heart's-ease from celestial spheres.

THE MOTHER'S PRAYER.

I.

WITH eager arms a mother pressed
A laughing babe against her breast.

II.

Then thus to Heaven she cried in prayer:
"Now even as his face is fair,

III.

"O Lord! keep Thou his soul within
As free from any spot of sin."

IV.

From heaven the Lord an answer made:
"Behold! I grant as thou hast prayed."

V.

Within her door the darkness crept,
And babe and mother sweetly slept.

VI.

The belfry rang the midnight bell;
The watchman answered, "All is well."

VII.

The mother, by the cradle-side,
Awoke to find the babe had died.

VIII.

With grief to set a woman wild,
She caught and clasped the marble child, —

IX.

Until her heart against his own
Was broken, beating on a stone!

X.

"O God!" she cried, in her despair,
"Why hast thou mocked a mother's prayer?"

XI.

Then answered He, "As I have willed,
Thy prayer, O woman! is fulfilled:

XII.

"If on the earth thy child remain,
His soul shall gather many a stain:

XIII.

"At thy behest, I stretch my hand
And take him to the heavenly land!"

XIV.

The mother heard, and bowed her head,
And laid her cheek against the dead,

XV.

And cried, "O God! I dare not pray —
Thou answerest in so strange a way!"

XVI.

In shadow of a taper's light,
She moaned through all the livelong night;

XVII.

But when the morning brought the sun,
She prayed, "Thy will, O God, be done!"

THE BROKEN VOW.

A WOMAN'S SOLILOQUY.

THIS spot is where we parted; and I think
That had he not turned back, to give the chain
That bound our hearts another golden link,
I might have suffered, when it snapped, less pain.
But, parting here, he loitered in the lane,
Then stopped, and, leaning on the garden gate,
He whistled like a robin to his mate;
Till I, with merry mocking of his call,
Ran down to meet him at the garden wall.

Uplifting both his hands, he seized a vine
And shook a storm of dew upon my hair;
Then, spying roses near, "O maiden mine!"
He said, "I pluck for thee a bud so fair,
That had it grown in any Eastern clime,—
Where love is writ in flowers instead of
thyme,—
And were it folded, thus, within thy hand,
Mayhap a woman's wit would understand
That her departing lover hies to bring,
With swift returning steps, her wedding-
ring!"

I heard, and trembled, and stood queenly
crowned,
But cast my eyes, bewildered, to the ground,
And asked myself, How could it be that I,
So lowly-born, should mate with one so high!

I turned my face to brush away a tear.
He bent his head, and whispered in my ear,
"Dear love, my loitering feet, so loth to go,
Shall speed me back before the bud shall
blow."

He went. That day was like a golden
dream—
And he the light that set the day aglow,
And I the mote that floated in his beam.

Then on the marble mantel of my room
I placed the bud, and nursed it into bloom,
And kissed the very thorns from day to day;
And yet the laggard truant staid away.
At first I saw the calyx swell and crack—
And break the promise of his coming back.

Then through the empty days, I asked
myself,
"Why comes he not?" At last the chilly
shelf
Whereon the fiery petals fell had grown
Like sandal wood for fragrance, or the stone
That pilgrims kiss within the prophet's tomb.
Outspread like pages of the book of doom,
The leaves too sweetly told my bitter fate.
His feet returned not to the garden gate;
His face I have not looked upon since then;
His name is written with the rich and great;
His fame is high among the famous men.
O Thou who sittest on the judgment throne!
Forbid my heart to harbor human hate,
But henceforth let me trust in Thee alone.

GOD SAVE THE NATION.

A WAR HYMN.

I.

THOU who ordainest, for the land's
salvation,
Famine, and fire, and sword, and lamenta-
tion,
Now unto Thee we lift our supplication —
God save the Nation!

II.

By the great sign foretold of Thy appearing,
Coming in clouds, while mortal men stand
fearing,
Show us, amid the smoke of battle, clearing,
Thy chariot nearing.

III.

By the brave blood that floweth like a river,
Hurl Thou a thunderbolt from out Thy quiver!
Break Thou the strong gates! every fetter shiver!
Smite and deliver!

IV.

Slay Thou our foes, or turn them to derision!
Then, in the blood-red Valley of Decision,
Clothe Thou the fields, as in the prophet's vision,
With peace Elysian!

THE STRANGE PREACHER OF PADUA.

A PADUAN Minorite lay deathly sick,
And cried, "O God! if I should die to-day
(Who thought to preach to-morrow), send a monk
With grace from heaven to pluck the church from hell!"

Next day at matins, while a thousand eyes
Were gazing at a shaft of fluted stone,
To which (as when a swallow builds her nest
Against a beam) the pulpit clung, uprose a monk,

Who said, "The holy friar whose face ye seek
Hath left his corpse outstretched upon his
bed,
And upward mounted to his crown in
heaven!
Be warned, O Paduans! turn and flee from
hell!"

As if he then had hurled a shaft of fire,
He stung their cheeks to scarlet, like their sin.
In anguish for their souls, some knelt and
prayed;
Some uttered groans; some faded ghostly
white.
Each sinner felt an earthquake in his breast.
And when at last the monk intoned the creed,
The choir were thick of throat — too choked
to sing;

The organ blew no breath through any
pipe —
The player's hands could only prop his
brows.
Then walked the stricken people from the
church,
As mourners mutely scatter from a tomb.

The preacher, with two friars, strolled out
beyond
The city's gate — their bare feet in the grass,
Their bare heads shaded by the orange trees,
Their voices answering to the lark's with
song.

Behind them followed — staggering, panting,
pale,
Scarce half alive — the priest they left for
dead:

Who, having learned the marvel of the day,
Sprang out of bed, made chase to catch the
monk,
Espied a club-foot underneath his gown,
And cried with voice that hushed their happy
hymns,
"O friends bewitched! I swear by Heaven
above,
This preacher is the Devil from below!"

With mildewed spots and warts, the preach-
er's face
Turned to a toad's — then changed and
seemed a monk's.

The brethren stared to see two human
shapes —
One risen out of death, one out of hell!

"O enemy of God!" exclaimed the friar,
"Before I strike thee with this crucifix,
Give answer why thou chidest men from
hell,
Since thou wouldst lure them in?" The
Devil quailed,
And said, "I warn men of their sins that
when,
Once warned, they sin again (as straight
they do),
Their double guilt shall bring them double
doom;
For at the judgment I shall say, 'O Judge!
The souls that charged their fall to trick of
mine
Speak shameless lies; — for, tempting not, I
warned;
And, snaring not, I pointed out the snare;

And, seeing them upon the burning brink,
With tears I bade them back; — yet down
they plunged!
Condemn them now to me, and to the
flame!'"

So saying, as a diver cleaves the sea,
He, diving, cleft the earth, and sank to hell.

With hands uplifted toward the city's
walls,
"O Padua!" cried the friar, "what tears
these eyes
Have wasted, weeping for your souls not
saved!"
Uprose he then sublime of stature, clenched
His hands, gave up the ghost, and fell a
stone!

All Padua, when it heard the tale, stood
dumb.
No man but vowed to live a whiter life!
O fickle human heart! Thy brittle vows
Are dashed to pieces on thy stony self!
The sinners sinned afresh! The Devil went
Not back to St. Antonio's church! No need!
For St. Antonio's church went back to him!

A VACATION HYMN.

ON CLOSING SCHOOL FOR THE SUMMER.

I.

WE sing a song, and then we part!
  How swiftly time is winging!
But sweet are farewells of the heart
  When they are said in singing.
The roses climb the garden wall;
  The buds have long been blowing;
The summer's breezy voices call,
  And we must now be going!

II.

The blue-bird trembles in her nest,
  Which every wind is swaying;
The robin sings and shows his breast,
  While we are here delaying;
The bees have set their pipes in tune
  On every head of clover;
And we must haste to hear them soon,
  Or summer will be over!

III.

O God of every lowly heart
  And every lofty feeling,
Be Thou adored for what Thou art
  In Nature's own revealing!

Wherever summer's grass is green,
  Or winter's snow is hoary,
The hiding of Thy face is seen —
  We know Thee by Thy glory!

IV.

If we who sing a parting song
  Have mortal meeting never,
There is a journey, short or long,
  Where summer lasts forever.
All hail, O fairest land of lands,
  Whose blossoms never wither!
Although we here unclasp our hands,
  Our feet shall travel thither.

FRIENDSHIP.

TO E. S. L.

O TRUE and noble friend! — (too far away:
Thou on the prairie, I beside the sea) —
The spring, that should be here, makes long delay,
And not a flower is open to the bee.
Meanwhile, from thee, the west wind comes to say,
Thy feet are walking where the fields are fair,
And nests are in the boughs that late were bare.
Thou hast the early season, I the late.

For thee the blossoms of the orchard blow ;
On me the sea-gulls and the fog-wreaths
wait.
But shall the leagues between us loose the
band
By which, though hands unclasp, yet hearts
may cling?
I ask myself, shall we, who, months ago,
Through frosty days, and in a frozen land,
Built up a friendship on the winter's snow,
Behold it melt and vanish in the spring?
False friendship was it, if it perish so:
True friendship is an everlasting thing.
There runs a record that not only saith,
He "loved his own," but "loved them to
the end."
So evermore a man shall love his friend,
With friendship that outliveth life and death!

THE HARP OF ANDREW MARVELL.*

"And if we would speak true,
Much to the man is due

"Who from his private gardens, where
He lived reservéd and austere
(As if his highest plot
To plant the bergamot),

"Could by industrious valor climb
To ruin the great work of time,
And cast the kingdoms old
Into another mould."

Marvell's Ode on Cromwell, 1650.

I.

O MARVELL'S harp! I dare to wake
Thy silent strings for Freedom's sake,
To sing how vain thy boast
Of Cromwell's conquering host!

* "These verses are an echo of Marvell's Ode to Cromwell. The Commonwealth of England, which,

II.

O Marvell's self! arise instead,
To warn the living by the dead,
How Freedom may be lost,
Though won at bloody cost!

III.

A nation, weak amid her might,
Sent forth her lowliest to the fight,
Until by men enslaved
The free themselves were saved.

by a successful war, was placed upon a sure foundation of freedom, was then, by an unsuccessful 'reconstruction,' set back upon the old corner-stone of monarchy. Let not the Republic of America, after a like struggle, suffer a like fate!" — *The Independent*, New York, Nov. 16, 1865.

IV.

But, O victorious state! — unjust,
Perfidious, false to Freedom's trust! —
Thy feet are trampling now
The men who crowned thy brow!

V.

Before the Judge of all the earth,
Men hold an equal rank of birth,
An equal law of breath,
An equal dust of death.

VI.

O Freedom! open thou a grave,
Where every king, where every slave,
Shall cast in crown and chain,
Till only men remain!

VII.

Meanwhile, I lay thee on the ground,
O harp! nor smite thee to a sound,
For now a poet's stroke
Is vain to break a yoke.

VIII.

But when the tardy earth hath rolled
Her kingdoms to the age of gold,
A poet by his song
Shall crumble down a wrong!

DYING AND YET LIVING.

I.

SHE died — yet is not dead!
Ye saw a daisy on her tomb:
It bloomed to die — she died to bloom:
Her summer hath not sped.

II.

She died — yet is not dead!
Ye saw her jewels all unset;
But God let fall a coronet
To crown her ransomed head.

III.

She died — yet is not dead:
    Ye saw her gazing toward a sky
    Whose lights are shut from mortal eye:
She lingered — yearned — and fled.

IV.

She died — yet is not dead!
    Through pearly gate, on golden street,
    She went her way with shining feet: —
Go ye, and thither tread!

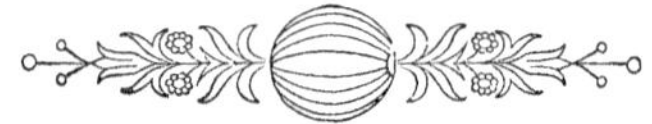

THE PRAYER OF THE NATIONS.

I.

O THOU by whom the lost are found,
Whose cross upon the mountain stands,
Let now its shadow on the ground
Spread east and west through all the lands
Until it wrap the earth around!

II.

O Christ, by this Thy conquering sign,
Let Thy extended arms outreach
To all who dwell from palm to pine,
To bind each human heart to each,
And all, O Crucified, to Thine!

III.

The morning stars give forth a song,
  But, like a discord in the strain,
The earth, through all her years of wrong,
  Forever moans as one in pain,
And cries, How long, O God! how long!

IV.

Yet not a star of all the sky
  To Thee hath fairness like the earth,
That rolls her zones before Thine eye
  To show to Heaven Thy place of birth,
And sepulcher where Thou didst lie!

V.

O Thou who cleansest men from sin,
  The Heaven of heavens, impatient, waits
Till round the earth Thy reign begin!
  O be ye lifted up, ye gates,
And let the King of Glory in!

IN MEMORIAM.

AN ACROSTIC.

THESE roses, planted on her grave,
have blown:
Her memory, still too fresh for graven stone,
Endures as written on our hearts alone.
O loving friend! when thee we hither bore,
Dim were our eyes, and black the weeds we
wore:
Our grief hath since grown less — our love
grown more.
Sweet gift of God! * whose gift we could
not keep! —
If ever angels watch where willows weep,
A wall of folded wings shall guard thy sleep!

* *Theodosia*, "Gift of God."

THE MONK'S MATIN.

I.

OUR night has vanished like a dream;
Too fast the witching hours flew by;
The moon too kindly veiled her beam;
We might have feared a clearer sky.

II.

We could not see each other's face,
For not a firefly lit a spark:
May Heaven forgive the mad embrace,
For we were blinded by the dark!

III.

Within our garden of delight,
  We thought the rose without a thorn:
And so we plucked the sweet at night,
  Nor ever felt the wound till morn.

IV.

The shadows bring the hours of bliss:
  The sunbeams that on lovers shine
Dry off the dews from lips that kiss,
  Till love is left but half divine.

V.

But could the joy be unrestrained,—
  And could the love go free of blame,—
O, would the midnight never waned,
  And would the morning never came!

MALTBY CHAPEL.

TO M. A. B.

I.

MALTBY Chapel, as you know,
Fell two hundred years ago.
Hardly now is left a stone,
Save upon the graves alone.
If your feet should chance to pass,
Weary, through the churchyard grass,
Rest them by a marble tomb
Crumbling over bride and groom,
Who, when they were hardly wed,
Found the grave their bridal bed.

II.

Flowering in the wall on high,
Like a garden in the sky,
Stood a window of the fane,
Whence, through many a rosy pane,
Lights of purple, blue, and red
Down through nave and aisle were shed.
Central in the fair design
Hung the Sorrowing Man divine;
Near him, gazing, knelt or stood
Mary's weeping sisterhood;
Next, with colors interchanged,
Holy emblems round were ranged,
First a light, and then a dark;—
Here the lion of St. Mark;
There the eagle of St. John;
Cherub heads with pinions on;

Virgin lilies, white as frost;
Palm and olive branches, crossed;
Picture of the Paschal Lamb;
Letters of the great I AM;
Last and topmost, Cross and Crown,
And a White Dove flying down.
Such a window, in the light,
Was itself a wondrous sight;
But the eyes that on it gazed
Saw devoutly, as it blazed,
Not the purple panes alone,
Not the sun that through them shone,
But, beyond the lucent wall,
Heaven itself outshining all!

III.

Up through Maltby's dusty road
Cromwell and his pikemen strode,—

Six and twenty hundred strong,—
Roaring forth a battle song;
Who, in marching to the fray,
Passed the chapel on their way;
Never dreaming how, inside,
Knelt a bridegroom and his bride,—
She the daughter of a peer,
He a knight and Cavalier.
Quoth the leader, "Rub the stains
Out of yonder painted panes!"
Glancing at a mark to strike,
Then a pikeman raised his pike,
Drew it backward half its length,
Hurled it forward with his strength,
Sent it whizzing through the air,
Sped it with a pious prayer,
Winged it with a holy curse,
Barbed it with a Scripture verse,

Heard it dash through pane and sash,
Till, above the tinkling crash,
Loud his shouting mates exclaimed,
"Bravo, Ironsides! well aimed!
So may every church of sin
Have the light of God let in."

IV.

Like the spear that pierced the side
Of the Saviour crucified,
So the weapon that was hurled
Smote the Saviour of the world;
Tearing out the sacred tree
Where he hung for you and me;
Curving downward, flying fast
Where the streaming rays were cast;
Flashing from the shaft each hue
Which it caught in quivering through;

Plunging toward the bridal pair
While they yet were bent in prayer;
Then, like very Death's own dart,
Pierced the maiden to the heart!
Back she fell, against the floor,
Lying crimson in her gore,
Till her bloodless face grew pale,
Like the whiteness of her veil!

V.

Years may come, and years may go,
Ere a mortal man shall know
Such a more than mortal pain
As the knight felt in his brain!
Long he knelt beside the dead,
Long he kissed her face and head,
Long he clasped her pulseless palm,
He in tempest, she in calm!

Stricken by his anguish dumb,
Neither words nor tears would come;
Till at last, with groan and shriek,
Brokenly he thus did speak:
"O sweet body! turned to clay—
Since thy soul hath fled away,
Let this lingering soul of mine
Lift its wings and fly to thine?—
Wed us in Thy Heavens, O Lord!"
Rose he then, and drew his sword,
Braced its hilt against the wood
Of the altar where he stood,
Leaned his breast against its point,
Stiffened every limb and joint,
Clenched his hands about the blade,
Muttered words as if he prayed,—
Then, with one ecstatic breath,
Cast himself upon his death!

VI.

Hence the tomb was made so wide
Both could slumber side by side.
But, though lovers fall to dust,
As their mortal bodies must,
Still, to souls that interblend,
Love itself can never end.

VII.

Rupert, flying in defeat,
Checked at Maltby his retreat,
Thought the chapel bullet-proof,
Camped his men beneath its roof,
Stood defiant for a day,
Fiery as a stag at bay,
Made a grim defence, but vain, —
Then, in darkness and in rain,

Fearful of the morrow's fight,
Stole away at dead of night.
When the Roundheads saw with rage
How the birds had quit the cage,
They, in spite, with blow on blow,
Fought the chapel for a foe!
So it came that tower and bell,
Roof and spire, together fell,—
Battered down, in name of Heaven,
April, sixteen fifty-seven!

THE FLY.*

A RHYME FOR CHILDREN.

I.

BABY Bye,
Here's a Fly:
Let us watch him, you and I.
How he crawls
Up the walls—
Yet he never falls!
I believe, with those six legs,
You and I could walk on eggs!
There he goes,
On his toes,
Tickling Baby's nose!

* These lines have been set to music by Lowell Mason; they may be sung also to the tune of "Lightly Row."

II.

Spots of red
Dot his head:
Rainbows on his wings are spread!
That small speck
Is his neck;
See him nod and beck!
I can show you, if you choose,
Where to look to find his shoes:
Three small pairs
Made of hairs—
These he always wears,

III.

Black and brown
Is his gown;
He can wear it upside down!

It is laced
Round his waist;
I admire his taste.
Pretty as his clothes are made,
He will spoil them, I'm afraid,
If to-night
He gets sight
Of the candle-light!

IV.

In the sun
Webs are spun:
What if he gets into one!
When it rains
He complains
On the window-panes.
Tongues to talk have you and I:

God has given the little Fly
  No such things;
  So he sings
  With his buzzing wings.

V.

  He can eat
  Bread and meat;
See his mouth between his feet!
  On his back
  Hangs a sack,
  Like a peddler's pack.
Does the Baby understand?
Then the Fly shall kiss her hand!
  Put a crumb
  On her thumb:
  Maybe he will come!

VI.

Round and round,
On the ground,
On the ceiling he is found.
Catch him? No:
Let him go:
Never hurt him so!
Now you see his wings of silk
Drabbled in the Baby's milk!
Fie, oh fie!
Foolish Fly!
How will he get dry?

VII.

All wet flies
Twist their thighs:
So they wipe their heads and eyes.

Cats, you know,
Wash just so:
Then their whiskers grow.
Flies have hair too short to comb!
Flies go barehead out from home!
But the Gnat
Wears a hat:
Do you laugh at that?

VIII.

Flies can see
More than we—
So how bright their eyes must be!
Little Fly,
Mind your eye—
Spiders are near by!
Now a secret let me tell:
Spiders will not treat you well!

So I say
Heed your way!
Little Fly, good day!

THE TWO HUNGRY KITTENS.

TO BE RECITED AT A CHILDREN'S PARTY.

I.

TWO Kittens grew hungry with licking their feet,
And ran around snooping for something to eat.

II.

"Me-ow!" said the Curly-tail, "milk would be nice."
"Ska-fitch!" cried the Smutty-nose, "*I* shall eat mice!"

III.

The house of the mice was a hole in the floor,
Too small for the kits to get in at the door.

IV.

So puss-in-the-corner they silently sat,
And waited awhile for the mice to grow fat.

V.

"Who comes?" cried a beautiful mouse, at her cheese.
The kittens replied, "We are rats, if you please."

VI.

"Not rats!" said the nibbler; "your paws are not pink,
Your eyes are too big, and your tails have a kink!"

VII.

"Come out!" quoth the kits, "and our tails
and our eyes
Will then look exactly the natural size!

VIII.

"Sweet mouse! we invite you to go to the
fair,
And you shall have plenty of combs in your
hair!"

IX.

The mouse said, "Excuse me, for I am
engaged!"
At which the two kittens grew fiercely
enraged.

X.

They flew at the mouse-hole, they awfully
squalled,
They fought one another, they tumbled, they
sprawled,

XI.

They twisted their whiskers, they tangled
their tails —
Then, scat! how they scampered to milk-
pans and pails!

XII.

The mice and the kittens no longer are
friends;
Which every one knows — so the story here
ends!

www.ingramcontent.com/pod-product-compliance
Lightning Source LLC
LaVergne TN
LVHW011236110826
845150LV00006B/1649

* 9 7 8 1 4 2 5 5 1 4 2 1 1 *